SEVEN SUPERPOWERS

SEVEN SUPERPOWERS

How Parents Can Shift from Punishment and Control to Comfort and Success

Copyright © 2022 by Dr. Maria Gilmour

All rights reserved. Printed in the United States of America. No part of this book may be used or reproduced in any manner whatsoever without written permission except in the case of brief quotations embodied in critical articles or reviews.

For information contact;

Wynne Solutions LLC
www.wynnesolutions.com

Dr. Maria Gilmour, author
www.sevensuperpowers.com

Book design and editorial by Bruce Miller

Illustrations by Gene Baz

ISBN: 979-8-9859731-0-5

First Edition: June 2022

SEVEN SUPERPOWERS

How Parents Can Shift from
Punishment and Control
to Comfort and Success

DR. MARIA GILMOUR
Ph.D., BCBA-D

CONTENTS

Contents v
Foreward vi
Note to Parents xi
Dedication 1
Introduction 3
Structure Zone 11
Delayed Gratification 25
Choosing the Right Bait 37
Total Recall 49
Patience Power 65
Fun Zone 77
People Presents 91
Acknowledgments 102
Author Bio 104
Seven Superpowers Flashcard 106

FOREWARD

Perhaps you picked up this book because your kids stress you out, or you're looking for ways to support their success. Maybe you always wanted a superpower, saw the cover, and asked, "Who is this Maria person?"

If you're looking for credentials, Dr. Maria Gilmour is a Board Certified Behavior Analyst at the doctoral level with over twenty years of experience working in developmental disabilities, including autism. She serves as the CEO of Wynne Solutions Behavior Services. She is also the Chief Clinical Officer of Gemiini Systems — the industry leader in on-demand speech, language, reading, life, and social skills training for those with and without exceptionalities. That's also where I work as Chief Executive Officer. I have served as a subject matter expert to multiple behavior analytic organizations, professional associations, health plans, and managed care organizations. This sounds impressive, but it's not the real reason to read this book.

The secret sauce comes from the fact that Maria and I have been friends for twenty years. Maria and I have enjoyed beer and hot dogs at minor league baseball games; she and my wife are best friends, and she served in my wedding and is my daughters' godmother. We have journeyed as friends, but our mutual desire to serve children with unique needs has kept us connected. We met through my wife, Andrea, who Maria supervised as a Board Certified Behavior Analyst. After that, Maria and I encouraged each other to progress from master's degrees to our doctorates in special education and now work together to develop evidence-based practices for kids with and without exceptional needs.

Maria and I share a mutual passion for supporting children who are misunderstood or shunted aside due to behavior issues. The learning labs for our methods were primarily clinical centers, but the ultimate proving grounds came from our family settings. Maria and I (and our spouses) similarly raise our kids using positive behavior support. Rather than reinforcing undesired behaviors with negative attention, demands, and yelling, we work to create the conditions for success. These include working with the child's strengths and interests, setting clear expectations at home, creating routines, and modeling the behavior you want your child to learn.

What's different about this book is that Maria has taken her years of academic training, clinical experience, and personal journey and distilled it into Seven Superpowers. She understands the fundamental challenge parents face during a tantrum or meltdown — that no one can remember a book's worth of parenting advice, but they can pull a tool from the seven tools in their belt.

Psychological experiments have shown that, on average, people can recall about seven items on the fly.

Psychologists discovered the "magical number seven" in the 1950s as the typical capacity of the brain's working memory. It has to do with how clusters of neurons fire in the brain. Maria wrote this book hoping that parents could keep these seven mnemonics in their brain's back pocket like handy flashcards to pull out in the store. They can be used while overseeing clean-up time or navigating a meltdown over a video game.

By the time you finish this book, you'll have access to seven simple brain hooks that carry rich associations. *Structure Zone* will conjure a picture of Maria's family bonding at the dinner table. *Fun Zone* will call up the love between daughter and dad at Disneyland as they outwit the kiddie height limit. And *Total Recall* will picture a red recording light on your kid's forehead every time you're ready to blow.

When Maria and I started twenty years ago, the thought of "professional" behavior analysts was a ways off — one thousand practitioners compared to forty thousand today. Back then, the primary support kids received was through special ed teachers. For a time, both Maria and I were special education teachers. Today, Board Certified Behavior Analysts are recognized as healthcare providers working in a wide variety of settings.

In that time, the basic science hasn't changed as much as the role of the parents and caregivers. One of Maria's clinical career hallmarks has been her ability to engage parents and caregivers to implement the program. Even if you develop the perfect care plan, a behavior therapist may only be with the child for a couple of hours a day. This puts the weight on the shoulders of parents and caregivers. They must be trained to establish a family structure for success and implement the consequences when things go off the rails. As this book makes clear, Maria is gifted in making parents comfortable in moving away from a punitive to a positive approach.

Today's families barely have the bandwidth to make and sit down together for dinner, let alone implement a behavior program. But more than trying to fit an advanced degree in behavior analysis into seven easy memes, Maria keeps bringing it back to the basics. The child needs to know that they are not alone and that their parents and caregivers are looking out for their best interest. She reminds us that even when the going gets rough, our children are people we love, and our kids need to feel that.

Please approach this journey as a co-partner with your child so that you can look behind the behavior to what your child is telling you. This is not an analytical skill but one formed from love. Try to remember that however your children are behaving, they are doing the best they can at that moment in time.

Bryan Davey, PhD, BCBA-D
CEO Gemiini Health

Note to Parents

Thank you for diving into the grand adventure of parenting with an open mind and loving heart. With these Seven Superpowers, I hope to inspire parents to manage behaviors with a positive and constructive approach that nurtures strong family relationships.

For some, this might mean getting your child to put away their toys or complete their lessons. For others, you might be facing severe behaviors that include aggression, property destruction, or self-injury.

If your family needs intensive support for behaviors, this book is not meant to be a substitute for professional help.

Please visit www.bacb.com to locate a Board Certified Behavior Analyst in your area.

Dedication

To my wonderful parents.

Thank you for guiding me

with your superpowers

and always supporting my dreams.

§

Children are people with their own needs and drives...

If you replace the phrase "inappropriate behavior" with "struggle for attention," it suddenly makes sense.

Introduction

The other night, I took my dog, Emma, to meet a new dog sitter. While I was there, one of the other dogs started yapping. I watched the caretaker take out a spray bottle and squirt the dog in the face.

"Whoa, what was that?" I asked.

"I just do this," the sitter gestured with the spray bottle. "The dog was barking, and now he's stopped."

I was stunned. "Well, we won't be doing that with my dog," I said. It was an awkward moment because I couldn't argue with the fact that the dog was quiet.

"Maybe it's effective for that dog," I said, "but that type of correction is not okay for my dog."

The sad truth is that it probably would be effective with Emma but also traumatic. I can't imagine taking her to that sitter ever again.

This is a parenting book, not a dog training book,

but the episode raised broader questions about appropriate behavior. We don't use a spray bottle on our kids, but every time our kids act, we react: We might yell, make threats, bargain, or lose self-control. As parents, our reactions can actually trigger inappropriate behavior in our children. Innocently, somewhere along the way, our roles as loving parents can morph into "kiddie-cops."

The dog sitter called his tactic "negative reinforcement," but he had it backward. If the dog barked every day at lunchtime when a passing train blew its horn, with negative reinforcement, you would bring the dog inside at 11:55 am. The goal is to maintain the dog's comfort zone. The technical term for the sitter's method is called *punishment*.

As a behavior therapist with years of working with kids and parents, I see how every child seeks a place of comfort. If they were puppies, you would cover their ears when the siren goes by – and if you don't, the puppy will howl. When kids express negative behaviors, they are telling us, "I need a place of comfort to feel safe and settled in myself."

All children process sensory input differently from their parents. Children on the autism spectrum process sensory input with even higher sensitivities. They may over-respond to some stimuli and block others. For example, they might manage their nervous system by fixating on a ceiling fan or squeezing into a tight space. They may stimulate their nervous systems by jumping, running, or flapping their hands. Or they might quiet their nervous systems by humming or rocking.

As adults, we also modulate our nervous system by going out for a run, taking a yoga class, phoning a friend, or sipping a glass of wine on the couch. These behaviors are appropriate – unless you sip that glass of wine on a couch at work. At the wrong time or place, all sorts of behaviors become inappropriate.

In the adult world, modulating our nervous system is called "managing stress." It's a bit unfair from a kid's point of view – they think, "Adults have a secret rulebook that says when I can run and scream and when I can't."

Even for seasoned parents, modulating an atypical nervous system with calm, measured responses is a challenge. For this reason, I've always wanted to put a "Parenting 911" guide into the back pocket of every mom or dad. I wouldn't expect parents to whip out the book during a meltdown, but if I could distill a stack of childhood theories into a handful of easy-to-remember precepts, parents could feel more confident raising their children in a difficult world.

I struggled through several different concepts for this book – at one point titling it "Warrior Mom." The Warrior Mom had seven magic arrows in her quiver, but the concept seemed too aggressive. Even the idea of superpowers can be problematic if you see yourself as The Hulk, who becomes ever more powerful as his anger boils.

As a parent, it's easy to feel that job number one is to

control. From wake-up to bedtime, you feel like the tyrannical boss of Family, Inc. with a hand on every control lever. As you become more seasoned in the role, you quickly realize that such control is an illusion. Children are people with their own needs and drives. What's more, our need to control behavior reinforces inappropriate behaviors. How is that possible? If you replace the phrase "inappropriate behavior" with "struggle for attention," it suddenly makes sense.

As a therapist, the number one thing I see in the home environment is too much attention to behaviors in general. This can be in the form of yelling, but it could also be much more benign, acted out of love and concern, and get overlooked by the parent. Explaining things in detail or bargaining with the child are examples.

- To the parent, it appears: "I'm the parent, you're the child, you're supposed to listen to me."

- To the child, it appears: "What about me? What about me? I need your attention."

Add a bunch of siblings and the struggle for attention multiplies. Attention is the currency of every parent/child relationship. Just like with cash currency, the parent's attention gives the child access to things – screen time, sweets, task avoidance, and so on. The struggle for attention lets the child manipulate the parent – outsmarting them to get their needs met. They have their own levers at Family, Inc. They know how to pull on their parent's heartstrings by crying or doing whatever works for them.

But it's not devious or malicious. Children are simply trying to get their needs met. And this is where I want you to pull up to 50,000 feet to objectively view the situation and see how a child's need for safety, comfort, and regulation of their nervous system is so innocent. That's why I would hug my stepson after he woke in tears from a nightmare.

Many of us need a hug when we feel scared. My stepson may have cried to get my attention, but that is okay. Can we see the innocence behind a behavior? Seeing that innocence helps us pause – to give a comforting hug or to redirect the conversation to something less scary.

In the struggle for attention, what is appropriate and inappropriate? Imagine you were watching a foreign language film filled with screaming parents and kids crying. You wonder, what's going on here?

They should send this brat to his room. But with your parenting superpower, you click the switch to turn on the subtitles and see the scene in a new light. The translation reads: *"Mama, my nervous system is out of whack. Please, I need comfort and regulation, attention and love."*

This book aims to be that switch – to read the family scenes in a new light. Here's an example:

When you see your child sitting comfortably on the couch, dog in their lap, and eating potato chips while watching SpongeBob, all seems well. But the same question arises: Is that appropriate or inappropriate? You might be starved for a few minutes of respite and be thrilled with the downtime, but that's not necessarily the best thing for the child. The child needs to build a level of comfort in their world – not from SpongeBob, but from you.

Changing your point of view from control and punishment to comfort and success seems monumental, but it doesn't take much – just one tiny shift in your thinking and perspective. It requires seeing the world through the eyes of the child. That's the switch.

Children act out of innocence – no different than a young puppy or a visitor to a foreign land. To set your child up for success, you will need to access their world and see it through their eyes.

Imagine that your child got on the coffee table inappropriately and started barking. Rather than reacting like that failed dog sitter, you might get up there with the child, offer a few barks of your own, and tell the story of Lady and the Tramp – how the Tramp barked all the time until Lady showed up. And then the Tramp felt safe and loved. Yes, that kind of Superpower.

This book is about creativity – not stimulating your child's creative forces but stimulating yours. The Seven Superpowers are designed to help you rise to the occasion. You have been blessed with an exceptional child. Your challenge is to invoke your superpowers as an exceptional mom or dad.

Superpowers are not punishments, control mechanisms, or behavioral change techniques. They won't bend the child's behavior to your will, either. But they will teach you to think on your feet, see the world through your child's eyes, and set your child up for success.

Superpowers will teach you to think on your feet, see the world through your child's eyes, and set your child up for success.

Instead of plywood, concrete, and 2x4s, a family structure is built from Consistency, Predictability, and Follow-through.

Structure Zone

"Maria, how was school?" my dad asked.

"My turn, my turn, I want to go first," Mikey blurted.

"The coach made us run extra laps," I said, "and two kids got in a fight at lunch."

"What about me?" Mikey tried again. "I went with Mom to the store."

"Fight any dragons today, Dad?" Karen chirped in.

"Brian?" my mom prodded.

"I dunno, school." Brian picked up his air guitar. "*Ba-ba-baba-bahh…* Stevie Ray Vaughn, *Little Wing*. Learned the opening riff."

"Wonderful," Mom beamed, always stressing the upbeat.

"My turn, my turn," Mikey insisted.

Welcome to my family dinner table. Sharing our day

with the family was a big deal, but with four kids, two adults, and slurpy eating, there was always a side dish of chaos with the spaghetti. No one cared about the mayhem because the power of our family dinner was larger than life. It didn't matter if I was riding my bike, climbing a tree, or listening to music with a friend; when the clock hit 6:00 pm, dinnertime pulled me like a magnet so I could race to my place at the table. We said our blessing, passed the food and ate as a family. I didn't get up without permission, and I cleared my place at the end.

When I share this story today, parents look at it me like I'm reciting a fairy tale or was living in a 1950s TV show.

"Hey, I'm happy if my kid eats," one parent confessed.

In recent decades, an increasing number of moms entered the workforce, takeout chicken or pizza in front of the television began to replace the family dinner. The pressure to work, commute, shop, cook, and deliver a wholesome family meal overwhelmed even the most dedicated moms. With after-school activities and sports, grabbing food on the go became more common.

Children enjoy a long list of benefits from the family dinner – good nutrition, conversation, expectations, and self-esteem. Driving it all is the number one superpower on our list: *The Structure Zone*.

My mom was a master at structure. As a kindergarten teacher, she taught her class how to sit, store their rugs, clean up, line up, and follow cues. Homelife seemed like a continuation of her workday, but she didn't seem like a kindergarten cop. Knowing what was expected of us kids removed a whole layer of anxiety that I observed in a more free-floating family environment. It's not that she ruled over us like a dictator; it is that she clearly provided expectations for nearly every situation imaginable.

My mom was like an ace pilot landing a plane in a storm. She and my dad created the flight plan for the family. They had the forethought for me to share a bedroom with my much older sister even though they could have converted a den for me. I think about this arrangement often. Maybe the plan was to put raw dough (me) into the proofing oven (my sister's bedroom), so I would rise into a perfect angel roll.

I'm no angel, but the proofing worked because I love my sister and always wanted to be just like her. If she did dance class, I did dance class too. She sang in the choir, and so did I. When she got a retainer, I pretended with a paper clip to have one, too. As we got older, she made the ultimate sacrifice and let me hang with her friends. And when we were old enough for dating, we rated each other's

boyfriends with stars – like critics do with movies. She only gave one guy a five-star rating – the man who became my husband.

Using the *Structure Zone* superpower, my parents saw how incredibly sweet, responsible, and smart my sister was, so I guess they hoped some of it would rub off on me.

When my sister went to study abroad in Italy, we remained incredibly close. There was no Skype back then, so we would compose two-hour cassettes talking about every intimate detail of our lives and send them back and forth across the Atlantic. That sacred pact continues. Every year, we take sisterly vacations together where we totally let our hair down.

Planting seeds for your child's future – *Structure Zone* is like planting seeds in a garden bed. You look into the future to see how the sun and space will foster growth. Thanks to my mom and dad, my sibling garden has continued to flourish.

Structure conveys many images – framing a house, parking structures, or studying the human skeleton. Unlike these physical structures, family structures are invisible. Instead of plywood, concrete, and 2x4s, a family structure is built from three things:

1. **Consistency** – the parent doing the same thing every time

2. **Predictability** – the child expecting or knowing what is going to happen

3. **Follow-through** – the parent delivering on the promise

As a child, the family dinner structure became firmly etched in my experience: Consistency (every night at six), Predictability (home-cooked food and not fast food in the car), and Follow-through (I clearly knew the rule or the consequences). Each of the three legs of the *Structure Zone* reinforces each other. Take away the schedule, the home-cooked meal, or the consequence, and the *Structure Zone* would collapse.

Consistency is more than dinner at six or a bedtime story at eight (but it includes those things). It also means that you respond to certain behaviors the same way every time. Because of consistency, the child knows that screaming for sugary breakfast cereals in the store guarantees a trip to the parking lot – even if the parent is time-pressed or bone-tired. Misbehaviors are less likely if there is no wiggle room in the parent's response. Good behaviors are repeated when the child receives consistent praise. These could be for sharing, cleaning up, or following directions. The parent's consistent response creates a positive *Structure Zone* around those actions.

> *Where consistency flows from the parent creating structure, predictability comes from the child knowing what will happen.*

Predictability follows from consistency. Where consistency flows from the parent creating structure, predictability comes from the child knowing what will happen. When your daily routines are predictable, your child knows what to expect for the day. There's no whining for a bedtime story if the day always ends with snuggling and a book. When your rules are predictable, your child knows how you will react to her behavior.

Follow-through means you will do what you say. Unfortunately, follow-through is usually presented as punishment – *"If you don't behave, you will be punished when we get home."* The true superpower comes not from punishment but from the comfort a child feels when mom and dad are good for their word. Instead of "If there's time after cleaning up, maybe we can get some ice cream," it's "Let's clean up and then get ice cream" – and ice cream happens.

Taken together, Consistency, Predictability, and Follow-through create a *Structure Zone*. The *Structure Zone* defines the routine you follow and the rules you live by. Structure helps parents and kids. Kids feel safe and secure because they know what to expect. Parents feel confident because they know how to respond, and they respond the same way each time. Creating *Structure Zones* makes daily life more predictable.

Structure starts with sleeping – People seem to bounce from one thing to the next in a busy day, but contrary to appearance, we actually function like well-tuned clocks. The natural cycle of day and night – or circadian rhythms – regulate our biological clocks. Our clocks are composed of specific molecules that interact with cells throughout the body. In fact, nearly every tissue and organ contain clocks that regulate hormone release, eating habits, digestion, body temperature, and more. When you experience jet lag after a trip, that's your biological clock disagreeing with the clock on the wall.

Our need for sleep forms the foundational structure of our day. When we turn out the lights each night, our brain starts its spring cleaning:

- **Dumping** the neural trash bin
- **Moving** memories into long-term storage
- **Clearing** the decks for new experiences

More importantly, sleep washes slow waves of cerebrospinal fluid over the brain to clear out the metabolic toxins built up during the day. This critical rejuvenation can only happen during deep sleep. Having a clear, open, and receptive brain explains why sleep is so critical to our kids' learning. Researchers have found that our brains retain 40 percent less information when we're sleep-deprived.

Creating a *Structure Zone* around sleep is not very

difficult. If bedtime is 7:30 pm, you allow thirty minutes to read a book, and the lights go out at eight. The magic of structure is that your child will start to get tired at eight o'clock every night. It takes some time to adjust if they are used to being wound up from TV and screens at night, but the rewards are significant.

Structure also starts with eating – Having regular meal and snack times also creates structure. If your children eat whenever they feel like it, they won't be hungry when it's mealtime. Importantly, food chaos causes stress and gets in the way of raising a healthy eater. It may also cause overeating. You play an essential role in shaping your children's eating habits by establishing where meals take place and what they eat.

Mister Rogers had this superpower – For anyone who watched *Mister Rogers' Neighborhood* growing up, you understand the magic of structure.

Every afternoon, Mister Rogers stepped through the front door with a smile and a song, took off his work jacket, and put it on its hanger in a closet. As a child, you could anticipate every move. From a hanger to the left, he pulled down a cardigan, put it on, and zipped it over his shirt and tie. Then he sat down to swap out his dress loafers for comfortable sneakers.

According to Hedda Sharapan, a director at The Fred Rogers Company,[1] "This predictability offered a sense of security. Through your rituals and routines, you're offer-

[1] https://wosu.org/off-air/importance-sweaters-sneakers-mister-rogers-neighborhood/

ing that to children, too."[1]

At the show's end, the sneakers went back by the bench, and the loafers came back out. The cardigan was swapped back for the jacket. The show ended as it began, with a smile and a song. Like the cycles of life, the rhythms of *Mister Rogers' Neighborhood* offered consistency, predictability, and follow-through.

Don't forget Big Bird – *Sesame Street* tapped into the same deep need children have for structure. As regular segments, The Word of the Day, Number of the Day, and the concluding *Elmo's World* all offered comfort in an uncertain world.

Let's Create a Structure Zone

A *Structure Zone* doesn't need to be fancy – If you encounter a small creek while hiking in the woods, you need a structure to cross it. You find a log for a bridge and a walking stick for balance, and you inch your way across. Creating a *Structure Zone* works the same way. You work with whatever is in your family life. The power of *Structure Zone* is that you can pull it out in an instant. Instead of "Go outside and play," with the superpower of a *Structure Zone*, you announce, "It's Bella's dog-walking time. Bella, ready to walk?" This works best if you put a schedule on the wall and the *Structure Zones* are enjoyable.

Create *Structure Zones* that follow you – Structures create cohesion, especially when you can pull out the structure when traveling or out in the world. Sitting together at mealtime is the place to start – even at a restaurant. Giving thanks for our food together creates connection and settles the energy. Waiting for everybody else to be served before you eat adds a structure. It also offers *Delayed Gratification* (we will talk about that in the next chapter).

Creating Rituals – Children love rituals. Baking a birthday cake, trick-or-treating, and decorating the Christmas tree form meaningful *Structure Zones*. The love of ritual continues into adulthood: throwing a coin in the fountain, enjoying the first pumpkin spice latte in October, or celebrating an anniversary at a certain restaurant. Parents can unleash their *Structure Zone* superpower by creating rituals from just about anything – silly or serious:

- Let the child invite two stuffed animals to join the bedtime story reading
- Hold hands before meals – even in the car
- Play a funny song sung by a cat on video during clean-up time
- Make a special moment to breathe and settle before entering a restaurant

Structure begins at any age – During their first year, young babies form a sense of trust in the world. If their needs are met with love, they form a basic trust that will form the core of their character. When the parent tunes into the structure of the home environment, even at a young age, the baby's nervous system gets into the *Structure Zone* and expects good things to happen. If you're wondering how to help your baby (or even your older child) develop this basic sense of trust, the answer is to recognize her needs and meet them with consistency and predictability.

Next steps – If your home life currently has very little structure, introduce change slowly. Begin by structuring just one part of the day, such as the time between dinner and bedtime.

Work with your existing family rhythm. If you have a natural order of tasks, turn them into a *Structure Zone*. Examples of this include finishing homework, taking baths, brushing teeth, storytime, and lights out. Organize your *Structure Zone* in a way that makes sense for your family.

Create a *Structure Zone* "command center" – Tape a large poster that lists each child's tasks as well as things you do together, for example, "Walking with Bella." If your kids don't read, create pictures of the tasks in order.

Expect some awesome gains, but remember that this can take time. It can take anywhere from a few weeks to a few months for children to become familiar with their routines. Eventually, the rhythm will become part of your children's lives, and they won't need much prompting from you.

Structure Zones should be fun, so be sure to add Storytime, Park Time, and Family Game Time.

Rules are meant to be broken (sometimes) – If you deviate from the rules, be sure to explain why you're making an exception. Maybe you all stay up late to watch a meteor shower or create a dog washing event for the neighborhood.

In the end, your *Structure Zone* will eliminate the power struggles, build family cohesion, and help your children feel secure and independent.

In the end, your Structure Zone will eliminate the power struggles, build family cohesion, and help your children feel secure and independent.

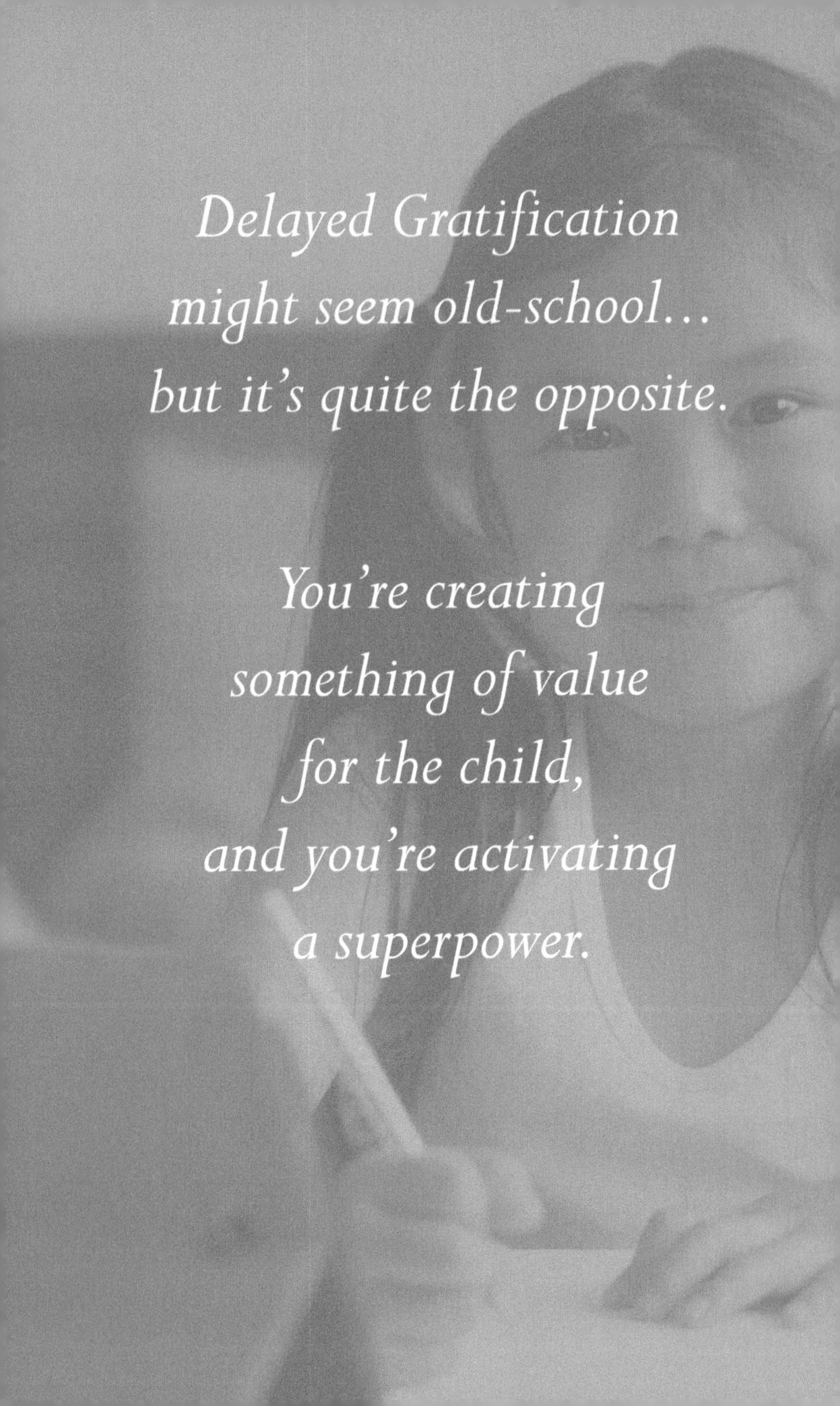

*Delayed Gratification
might seem old-school...
but it's quite the opposite.*

*You're creating
something of value
for the child,
and you're activating
a superpower.*

Delayed Gratification

From the moment you wake up – beep-beep-beep – to the moment you fall asleep, the ultimate IGD (Instant Gratification Device) lives in your hand – your phone. The apps and algorithms that live in your phone are designed to give you what you want when you want it, in just a couple of clicks.

Tap-tap-tap, click-click-click, like a bird pecking for grain, our phones feed an addiction for a certain kind of stimulation.

> "I feel tremendous guilt," admitted the Founder and CEO of Social Capital, while discussing social media with an audience of Stanford students. "The short-term, dopamine-driven feedback loops that we have created are destroying how society works."[1]

That may sound apocalyptic, but he has a point.

---

1   https://sitn.hms.harvard.edu/flash/2018/dopamine-smartphones-battle-time

Social platforms leverage the same neural circuitry used by slot machines and cocaine to keep people engaged. Instead of releasing a pile of coins, the slot machine in our brain releases dopamine – a rush of chemical messages called neurotransmitters. Think of them as reward pathways. They reinforce the connection between a stimulus or a behavior and the feel-good reward. Scratch a lottery ticket, win five dollars, and a neural circuit lights up.

The pull of dopamine – We don't think of our phones as Instant Gratification Devices, but the panic we feel when our phone is missing should give us a clue – peck, peck, peck – that continuous media feed keeps the dopamine flowing. Every few minutes another notification appears on Facebook, Twitter, Instagram, texts, and email. Peck-peck-peck. Is it a friend? A photo? An invite? Did I get a like? Wow, lots of likes! Every notification sends a flux of gratification.

If adults are nearly powerless against dopamine's pull, what about our kids? Children are powerless against candy, video games, and Santa promising a pony. And whether they own phones or not, kids are also beholden to immediate gratification stimulating their pleasure centers. But unlike adults, their needs are more primal. They want to feel safe and stay connected to their source of sustenance – and that's you.

It takes a superpower to overcome the pull of instant gratification – and only adults (teachers, siblings, and others) can model this resilience. It's not a strength you turn on by throwing a switch. It takes practice (a lot of practice). The ability to stay the course is a superpower that helps kids succeed in life. If they don't learn *Delayed Gratification* early, they will be forced to struggle with the same issues later in life.

Delayed gratification as a superpower – It was not by my choice, but my parents instilled the *Delayed Gratification* superpower in me in a big way. There was no cable TV and no Internet when I was a kid, though some friends had a Commodore 64 or Atari for games. I was allowed to watch my two favorite TV shows, *"Growing Pains"* and *"Full House."* This let me giggle with my friends about how cute Leonardo DiCaprio was during recess, but it only went so far. I was allowed two hours of viewing per week, Friday and Saturday. This meant I had to choose to record those two shows on VHS on Tuesday and Wednesday and delay my gratification until I could fixate on Leo and his cool hair for an hour on Friday and then "Full House" for an hour on Saturday.

My mom didn't read conventional parenting books.

She went against the grain of popular culture because she believed in ritual and structure. Back then, in a typical family system, kids would come home from school, turn on the TV and leave it on during homework, while on the phone, during dinner, and until bed. But not at our house. My mom even put a lock on the TV plug.

I spent my "free" time with extracurriculars – tap dancing, ballet, softball, and gymnastics. We came home, cleaned our rooms, sat for dinner at 6:00 pm, and then did our homework. It sounds harsh, but kids grow up in the world they're given. Eskimo kids don't think of their cold, dark winters as harsh; it's the world they know. In my world, we lived with this sense of time-shifting. Like dessert at the end of a meal, my entertainment goodies were served at the end of a productive week. From this, I learned *Delayed Gratification* at a young age.

Delayed Gratification might seem old-school – an eat your veggies approach to parenting, or even worse, a punitive type of thinking, but it's quite the opposite. For one, you're creating something of value for the child, and you're activating a superpower.

Delayed gratification powers success – Studies have shown that the ability to delay reward is present in highly successful people. It is a superpower that increases with age over our entire lifespan. As parents, we recognize this when a toddler throws a fit if asked to wait five minutes for a treat. The inability to delay gratification shows up with severe consequences later in life:

- Food gratification > Unhealthy eating habits
- Physical pleasures > Substance addictions
- Social neediness > Lack of academic achievement
- Impulse buying > Failure to save for retirement
- Inability to set goals > Lack of career advancement

A muscle to be exercised – Something as simple as a TV plug with a lock instilled a powerful learning in me. Today, screen entertainment doesn't need a plug with a lock. There are screens in our pockets, in our cars, on airline seat-backs, in every restaurant, and even on gas pumps. Video has become background noise. Rather than delaying gratification with the release of each weekly TV episode, you can stream-binge an entire season in a weekend. With so many IGDs, how do we practice our superpower? *Delayed Gratification* is an important muscle that must be exercised.

> *Delayed Gratification might seem old-school...but it's quite the opposite. You're creating something of value for the child – you're activating a superpower.*

It's easy to throw your hands up, "Fasting all week from TV would never work in our family. I need that downtime. When the kids watch TV, I can cook dinner, read a book, answer emails, or simply get off my feet."

Powering the parent – This takes us to the heart of the matter: The *Delayed Gratification* superpower is not for kids; it's for the parent. As a parent, we hold the superpower, and we make the decisions for our kids. The only reason *Delayed Gratification* is difficult is that it can be uncomfortable for the parent. We want to binge-watch Netflix. We want to look at our phones during a meeting or at church. We want to bargain incessantly with our kids to avoid family conflicts.

Building self-control – None of us signed up to be kiddie cops, but the parental mindset of laying down the law to control our children is the wrong picture. The goal of *Delayed Gratification* is to build a sense of self-control and will in the child by adding structure to the family's life. *Delayed Gratification* does not make a child rigid. It's a paradox – self-control builds a substance in the child that allows more freedom and independence.

The need for attention – When a child feels that they will always get what they want, they become locked into a cycle of immediate gratification. Just like with our phones, they become trapped in the need for this form of stimulation. But, this peck-peck-peck can never be truly fulfilling. It's a constant need for more sweets, more screen time, more attention, and more love.

> *This need for attention reflects a fundamental need to feel safe and secure in an insecure world.*

When this need goes unfulfilled, the child may feel more anxious and less secure. There can never be enough attention, and they need to feel secure.

Their need for attention reflects a fundamental need to feel safe and secure in an insecure world. *Delayed Gratification* creates comfort with uncertainty. Life unfolds the unexpected – traffic jams, doctors running behind schedule, a broken tooth, a high fever, a missing ingredient for dinner, a dead goldfish, and shipping delays at Christmas. When you learn to wait until Saturday for the Brady Bunch when you're nine, you become comfortable saving for a down payment at age twenty-five or going back to school when you're fifty.

The need for attention doesn't magically go away as we get older (for example, celebrities, and politicians). Consider teenagers. Their need for attention is social. People approach me and exclaim, "I can't believe you work with teens!" But I love how teens are so engaged with life. They're just trying to make sense of their environment which is their social world. Yes, they are difficult because they're going through complex physical and hormonal changes. But I look at them and think, oh my gosh, this is a different person from last year.

As a parent, you're likely talking to your thirteen-year-old like she's nine. Your assignment is to perform a mental reset and learn how to interact with your teen child in a new, more mature way. What does that look like?

A desire for social connection – Teenagers are different from any other age because they're going through complex physical changes, social needs and a strong desire for social connection. Suddenly, they want attention from peers, boyfriends, and girlfriends, which means we, as parents, lose our access to "child control." Their need for screens is not about distraction or gratification; they connect through apps and social media. This is a time for you, the parent, to update your *Delayed Gratification* rules and *Structure Zone* rules because you need to stay engaged with their development.

I learned a very big *Delayed Gratification* lesson during my high school years when my older brother got sick with a very rare disease. The *Delayed Gratification* superpower creates comfort with uncertainty, but this was more than I had bargained for. Our family didn't know whether he would live or die, and I didn't take it so well. Understandably, I was really emotional and had a hard time with the uncertainty. My brother was flown to the National Institutes of Health in Baltimore to be seen by the National Institute of Autoimmune and Infectious Diseases.

In the middle of this, something remarkable happened. I found I could remain in the uncertainty – it was a superpower. The uncertainty had been a killer at first, but after some time monitoring my brother's rare disorder, they ran an experimental treatment protocol involving a new regimen of medication for better long-term treatment and ultimately remission.

Remaining in uncertainty – *Delayed Gratification* builds the true superpower – resilience. Learning to remain in uncertainty builds a powerful skill in the child. It's a magical skill that can be applied to everything life sends our way. The good news is that you don't have to teach it – you only have to model it.

If we lose it, our kids are going to lose it. With so many pressures facing families today – wearing masks, vaccine decisions, telelearning instead of classroom time, deciding which settings are safe and which are not, avoiding parties, plus fires, floods, and winds from severe weather – our kids are watching us all the time and wondering, "Is everything going to be okay?"

In early 2020, at the pandemic's beginning, people went to crazy lengths to protect themselves – disinfecting UPS packages and hoarding toilet paper. Over the next two years, a strange thing happened. Even though each variant produced roughly 1,000 times more virus in the respiratory tract than the original strain of COVID-19, we did not become 1,000 times more panicked. We became more resilient, and we learned how to live with it.

A calm center – I can see the difference in families that model resilience. A calm center carries them through the center of the storm. I see kids waiting to talk without interrupting, getting their work done, and enjoying more quality family time. In families that operate with instant gratification, I observe high anxiety, over-stimulation, and talking too much in an effort to solve problems. Despite the frantic problem-solving, these over-stimulated kids are still not getting their needs met.

Modeling for your child – The path forward is to model *Delayed Gratification*. This means putting rules in place for the child and practicing them yourself. You may have to create an environment that supports those rules, and you may even have to lock the TV and deal with the reaction. So it's best to start with modeling. This might be as simple as a moment of silence to give thanks for our food before eating or letting each child finish their words.

As a parent, modeling might involve cutting out sugar – "Thanks for the cookie, dear, but I'm cutting back on sweets." Then talk about the experience. "You know, I was craving a cookie, but now I've lost my taste for sweets. I feel so much better." *Delayed Gratification* sets the pattern. Kids who eat healthier keep that model for life.

Walking the talk – We are taught not to follow people who don't practice what they preach. Modeling *Delayed Gratification* is as simple as that. As proof of this power, it's been adopted in corporate management jargon – "Walking the talk." And even more recently, in the language of organizational change, executives are tasked to "model the change in behavior you want to see."

Even if you feel ill-equipped to become the CEO of Family Inc., you've been given the promotion. Take the reins and turn your words into deeds. Your family will be grateful.

Even if you feel ill-equipped to become the CEO of Family Inc., you've been given the promotion.

Take the reins and turn your words into deeds. Your family will be grateful.

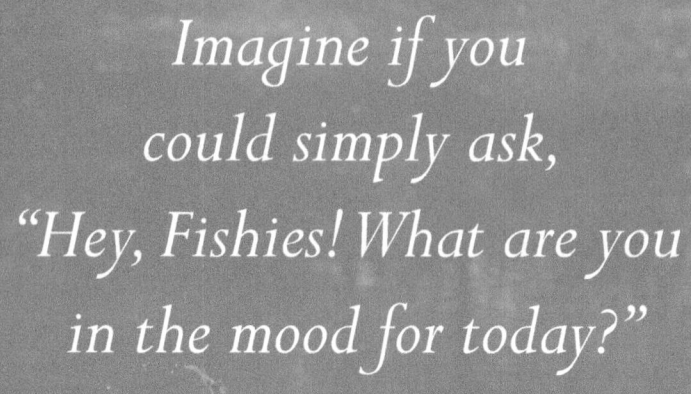

*Imagine if you
could simply ask,
"Hey, Fishies! What are you
in the mood for today?"*

Choosing the Right Bait

If you're a fisherman, step one is to choose the fish you want to catch and what it likes to eat. You consider the location of the fishing hole, the weather, time of day, and season. No bait works for every situation. Even if you spot schools of fish with sonar, choosing the right bait makes all the difference.

Imagine a world where you didn't seek advice from sonar, fishing guides, or experts. Imagine if you could simply ask, "Hey, Fishies! What are you in the mood for today?"

The bass is not going to answer "worms, please." But imagine if they replied, "It's dark down here. We want nightcrawlers!"

That would simplify fishing. There are probably even some old-timers who know how to talk to fish, but today's high-tech, Evinrude-powered fishermen don't think to ask.

The same holds true with parents.

Let me share a story. I was with my sister recently at a party in my house when Chad, my five-year-old nephew, threw a food tantrum. My sister (sensing my superpower) turned to me and asked, "Aunt Maria, you want to take this?"

My sister's nerves were on edge. I often get this assignment in such moments because I know what to do.

I took Chad into my office, waited for him to settle, and then calmly asked, "Chad, you seem upset. What would make you feel better?"

A minute later, Chad came out skipping and laughing. My sister asked, "Wow, what did you do?"

"I just asked him what he wanted."

"You what?"

"All I did was ask him what he wanted. He answered through his tears, 'I want cake.'"

"And I said, 'Oh, that's all you want?'"

"Yes, Auntie Maria," he replied.

"Okay. That seems reasonable," I reassured. "Let's have three bites of vegetables, and then we'll ask mommy for cake. And if we can have it, great. And if we can't have it, we'll find something else. Deal?"

Did Chad really want cake? Maybe he wanted cake plus attention from Auntie Maria. But rather than guessing or projecting my expert opinion, I simply asked him, "Chad, what do you need?" And we set it up.

SEVEN SUPERPOWERS

The miracle of attention – You might be scoffing, "So asking the child what they want is a superpower?" Not exactly. The superpower is *attention*. When I pulled Chad into my study, the focus shifted to just him and me. He had my undivided attention – mentally, physically, and emotionally, and he could feel it. Attention works like an energy transfusion: "Two-hundred mL Type A needed for Chad – "A" for Attention.

I learned about the miracles of attention – not from my grad studies – but from my little brother, Mikey. I grew up in an Italian-Irish family, but the culture was Italian. For an Italian child, the family meal means family and parents. It is a comfort zone that wraps everything with delicate warmth. In addition to providing stability and love, as we learned in *Structure Zone*, the meal is a time of sharing. I was lucky enough to embrace the sounds and aromas of the kitchen growing up, as well as the cacophony of laughter and conversation around the table.

If you're a little guy, like my brother Mikey, you're at a disadvantage at a loud and boisterous table. He wanted the Type A superpower, so he did the natural thing: He stood straight up in his chair and bellowed:

"HELLO!!! HELLLLLLOOOOO!!!"

Everyone laughed, but Mikey achieved his desired effect. We stopped and gave him our undivided attention. Mikey usually forgot what he was desperate to say because he really wanted Type A attention.

Attention does not require pulling Auntie into another room or standing on a chair. Later, as an adult, you don't need to run for political office to get grade A attention. Attention might come from a smile, making eye contact, or moving closer to the child. Proximity brings comfort, and even nonverbal gestures like a thumbs-up validate your existence.

Negative attention – Attention also comes in the Type N variety – Negative Attention. When a child baits the parent for negative attention, the child might be exercising the only way to break the parent's disengaged spell. After the outburst, the parent scolds, "I told you to stop it; do you hear me?" It looks ugly, but the food of attention – the eye contact and the engagement – is there, even if it's Type N.

If the bait is *attention,* we fail to realize that the child is not acting out of control. It's the parents who have baited the hook to reward anger. *The child learns that parents respond to tantrums.*

When Chad and I returned from my study, cynical parents might say his tantrum was rewarded. His cries and tears manipulated Mom and then manipulated Auntie, who delivered a piece of cake to shut him up. But when you turn the lens around, a different picture emerges. In the chaos of the party, Chad felt adrift without an anchor. If a boat pulls anchor in a stormy sea, the answer is to reset the anchor with a longer chain – not a tighter one. Chad didn't need cake; he needed comfort.

Reframing behavior – Imagine if you reprogrammed your parental response and replaced the phrase *"inappropriate behavior"* with *"struggle for attention."*

Instead of saying, "My child is being really bad right now," imagine if you didn't label behavior as good and bad. Behavior (whether from a child or an adult) reflects the nervous system in action. If a puppy chews your shoe or a kitten scratches the couch, they're not being bad; they need to exercise their teeth and claws. After you're finished feeling angry, and after your pet has endured "NOISE, NOISE, LOUD HUMAN NOISE," you recover your emotions and respond appropriately, "My puppy needs a chew toy; my kitty needs a scratching post."

> *Imagine if you reprogrammed your parental response and replaced the phrase "inappropriate behavior" with "struggle for attention."*

Imagine how different it would feel if you could say, "My kid needs attention."

Change the channel – It's normal to feel annoyed when your child is out of control. No one can always stay calm, and it's okay to react. But to exercise your superpower, you have to change the channel from *struggle* to *attention*. I work with moms and dads to help them see their kids like this: "I just want your attention, Mom. I'm just trying to get you to look at me."

Once you understand how you bait the hook for *attention,* the next challenge is to choose the right bait.

We use bait to engage the child because we want them to follow us. After asking Chad what he wanted, we agreed, "First we will do this, then we will do that." Chad followed my lead, but only because I listened to what he needed. He wanted cake.

It's no surprise that actual bait is a form of food. Food is incredibly powerful as a primal reinforcement, but what if the child is not hungry? There's a downside to using food as bait: Using food as a form of attention can create unhealthy habits and emotions associated with food later on.

Children at work – The actual bait for children is typically attention – in the form of recognition, warmth, safety, and love. At first, we use the bait to engage the child, and then we use the bait to capture their motivation. Children are curious, creative, and kinetic, and they are exploring their world and building a sense of self. Probing and exploring is their full-time job.

Watching for shifting interests – In a sailboat race, the skipper constantly watches the water for shifts in the wind. He might see the sail starting to luff or look down the course and see ripples on the water. An experienced sailor will anticipate a change in the wind's direction before it happens.

As your child grows, the winds of their interests constantly shift and become more pronounced until, *boom,* a sudden shift in their motivations will catch you completely by surprise. The bait for your big teen fish is completely different from the little bait you were accustomed to.

My mom was the master of anticipation at every age. She had a prize box that she kept hidden. When she wanted our attention, the box would come out. When we were little, the surprise box was magical. She knew when we wanted candy and when we needed to sleep. Her power to predict was like the mastermind of wind shifts. Where did she get this superpower? She had been a kid herself, so she didn't project adult needs onto little kids. She kept abreast of our motivations.

She knew that I enjoyed piano and dance class more than the softball team. She also knew that I enjoyed cross country more than playing basketball. As the skipper of the household, she kept a keen eye on the wind shifts.

Today, my kids enjoy karate more than soccer. Part of me would love to watch them

spend Saturday morning chasing the ball down the field like when they were a couple of years younger, but I am following their motivation. The *being* of the child knows what he or she wants. If you point their sails in that direction, you achieve maximum results.

Follow their passions – The Netflix documentary, *Count Me In* demonstrates the power of following your child's motivation. The film follows the passions and journeys of the world's greatest rock drummers. One scene features a home movie of the moment Emily Dolan Davies, now a professional drummer, screamed for joy as she ripped open her Christmas present at age six. She recounted:

For Christmas, I got an acoustic drum kit. And I remember falling against the wall because I was so overwhelmed. It was like giving me a lifetime supply of gold. I kept feeling this was the most incredible moment of my life! It was a sign from my parents, 'We believe you can do this, too.'"

> *Most parents lag behind their child's development. They're growing so quickly that it's hard to keep up with the rate of change.*

Unfortunately, most parents lag behind their child's rapid development. They're growing so quickly that it's hard to keep up with the rate of change. To access the superpower of *Choosing the Right Bait*, parents have to heighten their awareness: What are my child's wants and needs at this moment?

Like the superpowered fisherman, you can ask. Talk to them about their interests. Observe when they are turned on. Do more listening than talking. Give them choices to "collect data." That's what the professionals do. You won't be logging charts, so you will need to use your heightened awareness to observe what your child really wants.

Special attention with teens – When your child gets older, you must double your mastery of the wind. One moment my stepdaughter was a child, and the next, she yearned to become my trusted peer. Catching this shift is critical because you want your child to follow your lead – not *follow your command*. Even at the age when a teen "no longer listens to you," you are most effective as a model when you can capture their motivation.

Imagine you are a sailor: "Oh, the wind is shifting starboard; let's tack and sail where the wind is taking my child."

I observe this shift with my 14-year-old stepdaughter every day. She knows exactly what I want her to do so she can get what she wants. She loves to watch TV shows with me – especially stories with more mature themes. Why is that? Because she is maturing and is attracted to the mature world. I grew up with a physical lock on the TV plug, so I'm more like my mother and more strict than modern parents. I don't want them to watch R-rated movies, so I review the movies before our snuggle time on the couch.

Coveted time – My stepdaughter and I avoid the

push-pull of what she gets to watch. We avoid the power struggle through the superpower of the magic bait. She loves the attention she feels in her coveted time. Even when I fast-forward through inappropriate scenes that I previously spotted is not a cause for push-back. She recognizes that my investment of energy makes our shared time special. And so she will invest as well. She will do her homework, practice her kickboxing, clean her room, and take a shower. Once the boys have left for karate, she will be waiting outside my door. She knows she's earned it.

My stepdaughter has also learned *delayed gratification*. Yesterday, at our coveted time, my parents called, and I ended up being on the phone for two hours. So she had to wait two hours (and so did I) – even after doing all her get-ready work. But she knew what to expect.

Our child might not be a star soccer player, even if that was my dream. I wanted to give birth to a little boy with a strong left kick. If you don't play soccer, this might seem crazy, but a left-footed player has superpowers of his own. That didn't happen. But instead, I learned to stay abreast of their interests so that they can develop their talents without cross-currents from parents.

All children have individual superpowers, and your job is to recognize those powers and help them ignite. You can't create a lefty, but you can create opportunities for the writer, builder, mechanic, or musician to find their calling.

Tapping into their motivation – You follow their motivation because you want your child to be excited about the path they discover. Today, little Mikey and I are both in helping professions. We both discovered our inner motivations to go to work and talk with people and support change in their lives. It's something we enjoy. Sure, it's taken a lot of work to get advanced degrees and set up practices – but the superpowers of structure, delayed gratification, and following our motivations paid off. I hope to go back to school and continue to grow.

You may have read this chapter and come away with the feeling, "How can I follow my kids' motivations? They seem all over the map!"

Instead of a plastic worm on the hook, try something new to engage their curiosity. If your children aren't exposed to new experiences, they won't know if they like to play soccer or work with wood or program computers. So it's okay to pair soccer with a favorite restaurant afterward – yes, a ritual of *Structure Zone*.

Setting up success – Expose your child to new things, but remember that successful fishing means following their lead. That's how you set your children up for success.

*Your child is watching you at all times —
taking cues from how you handle life events, learning how to react under stress, recording household language, and forming biases.*

Total Recall

In the 1990 film, *Total Recall*, Arnold Schwarzenegger receives an implant that fills his brain with memories as a secret agent on planet Mars. It's never clear to the audience whether the story on the screen is real or a false implanted memory. The philosophical questions of appearance versus reality and the nature of memory elevate *Total Recall* from an exciting action flick to one of the most mind-bending sci-fi films of all time.

What does this have to do with raising kids? Because we, as parents, implant formative memories in our children.

Imagine if your child wore a body-cam that recorded every word and action in the household – from wakeup until bedtime – and that this recording was archived into their "permanent record." It sounds scary, but this is pretty close to the case. As parents react to one family crisis after another, we overlook the memories being planted in our children.

A permanent record – When I was a kid, the idea of a "permanent record" hung over me and my classmates' heads at school. Parents and faculty would threaten that our misbehavior would go onto our permanent record. This would be horrible because – being permanent – it would follow us through life.

Like a sponge – While the ominous threat we received at school was oversold as a corrective measure, there is, in fact, a different kind of permanent record. A child's brain is like a sponge, absorbing everything that goes on around them. Every little thing they soak in builds connections in their brain to shape their fears, expectations, and needs.

The rate of absorption in a child's brain is staggering:

If we compare our ability as adults to that of the child, it would require sixty years of hard work to achieve what a child has achieved in these first three years." ~ Maria Montessori, *The Absorbent Mind*.

The child's absorbent mind captures complete images that become fixed in the subconscious. There is no filtering or discrimination. The sponge-like mind records the events and impressions from its childhood years as it grows into the reasoning mind of an adult – but always retaining these sights, sounds, and words recorded from childhood.

Look who's watching – Put more bluntly, your child is watching you at all times – taking cues from how you handle life events, learning how to react under stress, recording household language, and forming biases. Your child even absorbs and records the tone of your voice. This is not child development theory; you can observe it in every moment.

For example, when I speak to our dog, Emma – the one who almost went to the squirt-bottle guy – I adopt my sweet, mommy tone of voice, praising her, "Good girl, Emma." Well, guess what? My husband, with his resonant radio voice, and my stepson, with his deep, changing, adolescent voice, both praise Emma in my sweet, mommy voice, "Good girl, Emma." Proof that the sponge absorbs everything and continues beyond age three.

Instead of "Good girl, Emma," consider how snapping, yelling, and fighting fill a tense household and how the child's sponge absorbs that negativity. Or, using another metaphor, the child's "body cam" is recording pictures of how to talk, relate, and respond to others.

The body cam is not just a metaphor. Before the pandemic, we wore GoPros when we worked with families to record their interactions. I even tell the parents I work with to pretend they're wearing a camera. Act as if anytime you're with your kids, it's being recorded.

Children let us know that they are "recording" by reminding us of things we have no memory of:

"You said we could go get ice cream if I walked the dog."

"I did?"

Or, "Remember when you said my hair looked like a bird's nest?"

"I said that? I must have been joking."

This may embarrass you or raise concerns about memory loss, but our children let us know that they're listening – even if they appear not to be paying attention. Over time, you'll see them repeating words, mannerisms, and reactions.

This can get crazy. When I was a child, my dad, being a natural comedian, would say in his fake Italian accent "ah-Mamma-ah-Mia!" (with hands in the air like he was conducting an orchestra). Whether his "Mama Mia" came from the Abba song, or the classic Alka Seltzer commercial ("Mama Mia! That's-a one spicy meatball!"), I don't know. With his infectious sense of humor, my dad escalated again, repeating this rhyme to us, "Mama Mia, Papa Pia, Baby's got the diarrhea." We laughed hysterically.

I told this story to my kids while we were driving from Seattle to Portland. No surprise, potty humor is a big hit with adolescents. What's more, because Grandpa said it, that gave them license to put the verse on auto-repeat – and they did. Eventually, I had to reel it back in by discussing the propriety of singing about diarrhea in public.

Your children are watching, and the camera is forming a permanent record. So, how do you turn this into a superpower?

Your children are watching, and the camera is forming a permanent record.

You are the director – Continuing the filming analogy, you're the director of this story – always directing the scene. Imagine you're Steven Spielberg: "Places everyone. In this restaurant scene, we will have a polite conversation, follow your parent's lead on what to order, and be attentive to the server and other patrons."

The director does more than react to the action. In filmmaking, the director rules the set. She sees the plan for the day, blocks out the action, follows the character development, and knows when to say, "Cut!"

From a filmmaker's guide:

> Everyone on set is expected to adapt to the rules of the game. This means accepting announcements as binding. Even if a crew member doesn't immediately understand a director's announcement, you can be sure it will be backed by experience and common sense. If every crew member questioned every announcement, the progress on set would be virtually zero.

I particularly like this advice:

> This understanding amongst everyone working on the production sets the tone on the set and gives the director the space they need to focus on their creative work.[1]

Conscious modeling – How do you set the tone on your family set? Instead of blocking out shots and calling "action," the parent is modeling behavior. At the most basic level, parents who gulp sodas and chew jellybeans while watching TV are modeling behavior. The same holds true for cigarettes, alcohol, physical punishment, cursing, agitation, and all the rest. This is unconscious modeling.

Conscious modeling does not require forgoing jellybeans, chanting "Om," or delivering teachable moments. Conscious modeling is simple, but also your superpower:

---

[1] https://yamdu.com/en/blog/the-nine-things-filmmakers-need-to-know-about-etiquette-on-set

SEVEN SUPERPOWERS

Just be aware that the camera is on. If you've ever been on stage in front of an audience, you make adjustments. Your posture straightens, tone and diction improve, and you make eye contact. You also smile. Awareness that the camera is on cleans up your act.

Like all things, conscious modeling is easier said than done. Camera-awareness requires self-awareness. People who pray, meditate, study yoga, practice tai chi, or work with a therapist all seek self-awareness: "How can I decouple from my reactions and unconscious behaviors?"

> *Like is all things, conscious modeling is easier said than done. Camera-awareness requires self-awareness.*

Managing the leash – If you train a young dog to walk on a leash, the camera is on. You can't space out, enjoy the trees, or talk on your phone. All that doggie energy requires your full concentration and self-awareness to control the leash. You are modeling behavior: "Fido, this is how we walk on a leash." Fido learns how much slack, sniffing, barking, and marking are appropriate on a walk.

As a kindergarten teacher, my mom had a superpower for modeling. She could choose which behaviors to model for our permanent record. When I was young, her friends would gather at McDonald's for morning coffee and gossip. They had a lovely time, but my mom made a conscious point not to join their coffee klatch because she did not want to model gossipy, catty behavior. She didn't make lessons out of it, but her modeling affected me. I was never part of any cliques when I was in high school. Instead of feeling isolated, I was quite popular because I was friends with everybody.

My mom also modeled how to stand up for what you believe in. For a young girl, this is an enormous superpower. I received this superpower at an Olive Garden restaurant which is funny because Italians consider the chain to be "fake Italian." But my lesson was not about cultural authenticity, it was about our right to eat without cigarette smoke.

The Olive Garden lesson began when my mom asked to sit in the non-smoking section. The people in the adjoining section were lighting up clouds of smoke, so I looked at my dad and could see his stress level go up – not from the smoke, but because my mom was motioning to the manager. I got nervous because I knew what was coming.

"This is not okay," she declared. "We asked to be seated in the non-smoking section, and clearly, there is smoke coming into our faces. Either you remedy the situation, or we will leave."

California was the first state to enact a statewide smoking ban for restaurants, and I like to believe that my mom played a role. Many times, we all got up and headed to the door. But I learned from her to be strong, state my case, and not be afraid of what others might think.

That was the moment I learned to advocate for myself. I was ready to dig into the breadsticks, but my mom's tone and self-assurance pushed me to the edge of discomfort. My camera went on as I observed how she didn't go over that edge. Her self-awareness kept her assertion perfectly balanced without self-entitlement or making a scene.

Ready, action – Conscious or not, the camera goes on whenever there's a swing of emotions. When Mom motioned to the manager, we watched intently: What is going to happen next?

When you sense a burst of emotions, high excitement, or significant stress, this is an indicator that the child's body cam is on – almost like a little red recording light on your kid's forehead. It doesn't matter if it's an emotional outburst or a teaching moment; it's being recorded.

Kids take particular notice when the volume of your voice increases. Suppose you're from an Italian family (like mine), and it's always loud? I go into some homes where high decibels prevail – just constant talking, louder and louder:

"Did you guys feed the dog? Do your homework? Wash for dinner? GET YOUR BUTT DOWN HERE!!"

Tuning out – If that volume is constant, the camera can shut down, and the child can go numb. That's why yelling at your kids repeatedly is not effective. Your message becomes white noise to them, and they ignore it. And if you're snapping, they start snapping. You're teaching them how to react when you're in a high-stress state.

Down-shifting emotions – I'm not a Zen master at mastering my emotions. For example, I stress every time I talk to a health plan. In my practice, we work with severe behaviors. Amid the stress this morning, while frantically gathering materials for a client matter, my husband came into the office and said gently, "Let it go. Let's have a little time with the kids."

"I can't be around the kids right now," I said. "I don't want them to see me so stressed out like this."

So, he wisely left so I could let off some steam. He motioned to the kids. "Hey guys, let's go to our rooms and read a book for a few minutes."

I just needed a couple of minutes. Parents need to know when they shouldn't be modeling behavior for their kids. When I have high levels of stress, which happens often, I stay in my office until I can change my mood. I might let them know I need a little space. Being able to take a step back is a superpower.

Parent time out – We are familiar with "time-outs" for our kids, but a parent time-out is equally important. With that kid camera on, you want to be able to "think, then act." Taking a pause – lots of pauses – will help you set the tone on the set. I have little signs in my office that read, "Ten minutes of calm, then time to talk." I give them to my clients. Ten minutes is a long time. But for parents dealing with high-level, severe behaviors, everyone should pause a beat before they engage.

Let me share two more Mom stories:

First story – When I was six years old, we took a family vacation in a motorhome. At the end of every day, each child in the family created diary entries of our travels in a scrapbook. I was a good sport about this, except the one time I resisted the task.

I share this story because it is firmly implanted in my permanent record. I can still see my dad driving the rented motorhome with his Top Gun sunglasses, plaid shorts, and a polo shirt with the little alligator. My mom sat with me at the table, teaching what has become a professional skill – the art of follow-through with a non-compliant child. Six-year-old me had no idea that I would pull this teaching from my *Total Recall* to guide my career.

"Aarggh! I don't want to!" I objected.

With hostages, you can spot signs of a forced video

confession and acts of resistance. In my case, this meant pushing the pencil so hard it broke through the paper. I also scribbled haphazardly to ruin the page.

My cool, calm, professional teacher mom ignored my outbursts and attempts to wriggle out of the task. She kept redirecting each outburst toward the task, one word at a time. She even ignored my strident acts of resistance, the scribble, and scrawl of pencil marks all over the paper. She kept returning my attention to the page, "Okay, and after that what do we do?"

I blurted another "aarggh."

"Keep writing, Maria," she replied. Her calm, matter-of-fact toned offered no escape.

With all rhetorical exits blocked, I couldn't get off the hook. My non-compliance only invited love, as if she was feeling, "Oh my little Maria. You are okay, and you will get through this. I'm going to help you."

That was one of Mom's superpowers. When she would tell us, kids, "I'm going to help you" or "let me show you," you could feel your defiance melt.

At first glance, my mom might seem stubborn – like a battle of wills. But her superpower resided in her ability not to get triggered by my behavior. I knew she wasn't heartless – even when I looked at her with tearful eyes. My scribbled defiance was strong, but her perseverance and heart were stronger.

After thirty minutes of white-knuckled resistance, I changed gears and wrote my recollection with perfect handwriting. A wave of emotions from Mom's superpower brought me to a calm and peaceful state. She demonstrated that we can get the work done and do it beautifully even when we are emotionally charged.

The second story involves the Aesop fable, *The Boy Who Cried Wolf*. Aesop was a slave who lived in Ancient Greece. I can only imagine that his captivity gave him a deep sense of morality and insight into human nature. Aesop mostly used animal characters in his tales – perhaps to soften the harsh lessons. Classic children's tales might involve poison apples or wolves with terrible claws and teeth. Even *Ring Around the Rosie* is about the Bubonic Plague. Children have the capacity to touch these dark places, and my childhood nightmares bear this out.

Before I had nightmares, I was an attention-seeking child. This is not unusual when you have older siblings. My parents and siblings gave me anything I wanted as a baby. I could point at something, and boom, they would respond.

I enjoyed being at the center of their world until Mikey was born. Suddenly, I was no longer the star of the show. As Mikey explored the world with his cute baby voice, the three of us older kids would "ooh" and "ahh" and adore everything he did. But all this time, I craved my former role as the center of love and attention in the family.

I didn't choose nightmares as a way to reclaim the spotlight, but that's what happened. The Disney film *Fantasia* deeply impacted my subconscious, particularly when

Mickey Mouse becomes a sorcerer. With dark foreboding, Mickey conjures cosmic spirits to animate brooms and pails and deliver floods of water.

Mickey's sorcerer magic didn't end on the screen; he came into my bedroom at night, hovering larger than life over me. My cries of distress pulled my dad to my room to comfort and hug me. One time he even brought me a little teddy bear.

How I savored this attention, and now I knew how to get it! I had unlocked the formula – nightmares are rewarded with special time with Daddy.

"Daddy! There's a scary monster in my closet!" or "Daddy, there's a giant spider in my room!" or "Daddy! An evil mouse is haunting me from under my bed!"

I don't know if my parents discussed my nightmares, but my cool-as-a-cucumber mom saw through the theatrics. She sat on the side of the bed and told me the story of *The Boy who Cried Wolf*. I don't have to repeat it here, but suddenly my spiders, monsters, and evil mice were stand-ins for the fictional wolf. Mom's simple logic evaporated the dark world I had summoned into the light. I didn't give up my ploy immediately. It took a few of these lessons for her superpower of modeling a new grown-up behavior to transform my inappropriate attempts for attention.

Everyone seeks attention – All "kids" (young'uns and grown-ups) seek attention – in short, *to know we're loved and cared for*. This need, if unmet, follows us doggedly through life. This fundamental need to know that we are unconditionally loved, if missing, can distort the choices we make, the people we fall in love with, and the paths we follow later in life.

"Crying wolf" was a cry for attention for the young Maria, especially with my new baby brother grabbing the limelight. Fortunately, my parents had the superpowers to navigate my needs, and I had the *Total Recall* to take it in.

As you will see in the chapter *Fun Zone*, my mom and dad knew how to show me that I was still loved in a special way.

Few of us understand that patience is something to be exercised, and when you do, you develop a superpower — and your kids do too.

Patience Power

In 1979, Federal Express launched the groundbreaking concept of overnight delivery with the tag line, "If it absolutely, positively has to be there overnight…." By the 1980s, instead of overnight, a document would transmit into your fax tray in just a few minutes. By the 1990s, AOL users were greeted with "You've got mail." Flash forward to now, and 85% of the world's population receives instant smartphone messaging throughout the day.

The speed of technology has delivered a productivity boom. What's been lost is patience.

Few people remember the anticipation and delight of opening the mailbox to find a love letter scribbled with little hearts on the envelope. Even waiting for a film's theatrical run to finish before you can watch it on TV has become quaint. Few of us understand that patience is something to be exercised, and when you do, you develop a parenting superpower — and your kids do too.

Like all my superpowers, my *Patience Power* was bestowed by my mom and dad. Am I grateful? Yes. Did I like it? Hell no.

This story might make you squirm. If so, I apologize in advance.

I grew up in coastal Southern California, a lush paradise overlooking the sea. My tight-knit group of friends lived freely amid the natural beauty of scenic bluffs, sagebrush, and trails to the oceanside. When high school beckoned, we were eager to blossom together at the public high school. But that's not what happened.

One afternoon, after school, my mother informed me, "Your father and I have been considering your future, and we both feel that you would be best served at a private high school. We feel it is the best scenario for you."

This may sound reasonable, but they could have been sending this beach girl to Kazakhstan or even Mars. My high school was a Catholic, all-girls high school taught by strict nuns. That's strike one. Then add two hours of commuting each day on the fearsome Interstate 405. Finally – and most devastating to a 13-year old girl – all of my friends (my tightly-clung world) were heading to our neighborhood public high school. When you're 13 or 14, your whole world is relationships you're building with your circle of friends. Adding to the injustice, my older sister went to the local public school, and as I mentioned before, I wanted to be just like her.

I think my mom feared I was rambunctious and boy-crazy and would never buckle down. Or maybe she had the crystal-ball power to see my future. Today, she remembers that I was a really difficult teenager, but I had no idea how difficult I was for her.

I pulled out the predictable rant straight from my 13-year-old-girl script: "The answer is no; I hate this school; I don't wanna go; I wanna go to the high school right down the street and be with all my friends, my very best friends. This is the end of my life!"

This was a horrible, life-altering decision for a young teen girl and the worst time to make it. But coming from my parents, their certitude felt like an immovable rock. I felt their resolve without words or discussion. They stood firm in their stance: "This is what we're doing. We're going to be patient through Maria's tantrums for the next month, or maybe three months, or as long as it takes." They must have stocked emotional provisions to ride it out.

> *I'd never doubted my parents, and I found comfort in the rock of their certainty.*

This is where the story might appear confusing. I'd never doubted my parents, and I found comfort in the rock of their certainty. When they dropped this bomb, I tried to manipulate the situation to see if they would relent, but they didn't. I was spinning my tires in the mud. You know it's fruitless in that situation, but spin you must.

An immovable nature – If this were a movie, the family would scream until red in the face. But, there was no screaming except for the daily "Maria, come down to dinner." This level of calmness seems unheard of in an Italian household. Like most kids, I dug in my heels to feel the immovability of the rock, the comfort from the rock, and to take a measure of what I was dealing with.

What happened next seems like one of those feel-good movie scripts. I had always believed my parents; I just didn't like it. After a couple of months, I stopped moping and decided to get involved — at first, some clubs, then the social scene, the student council, and then my studies.

I was actually starting to enjoy myself.

Like a rock! – When I was running cross country, I realized that, wow, mom has a patience superpower. I met some super cute boys from our nearby "brother school", our fellow all-boys school, and I thought, "This is cool; I can survive this." And when I was elected president of my class, I felt, "Mom, you rock."

People remark, "Your mom is amazing. I could never rip my child from her world nor deal with the push-back." It's true — ripping your kid from her world and putting her in a car for two hours on an LA freeway when she's meant to be blossoming could be setting the stage for a horror show. What parent would subject that much emotional stress unless they had a long-term vision for their child's success?

Enduring the blowback – I had friends whose parents also sent their kids to private schools — but without the rock of solidity. Their parents pulled them out because they did not have the *Patience Power* to endure the blowback.

Now that I consult with families professionally, I understand that it would not have worked if my mom had just declared, "you are going to an all-girls school," without a larger vision she and my dad had for me. To build my trust at that critical moment, they had already made a long-term investment — like a soul project. From the child's point of view, the rock of solidity is built continuously — it is built from patience.

When I work with clients, we first run assessments to determine the reason for their child's behaviors. Then we educate the parent how to respond once they turn on their *Patience Power*. We tell them to get ready for a huge spike — the blowback. The behavior might very well become more intense than you've ever seen, and you have to be prepared. We might have to take all the furniture out of the house with extreme behavior and literally take everything off the walls. We explain that the acting out could go on for several nights. Here's how *Patience Power* works:

The fuel of attention – You cannot reinforce spikes in behavior by giving it attention. Attention fuels the push-pull that reinforces behaviors. When the parent stops feeding tantrums and behaviors with attention, the parent expects magic; they expect everything to calm down. But instead, the initial *Patience Power* produces an even bigger flare-up. This is the critical point where the *Patience Power* gets exhausted.

"YOU'RE RUINING MY LIFE. I WILL NOT GO TO THAT SCHOOL! NO WAY, NEVER!"

I'll explain to clients, "You'll see a huge spike." Many

parents can't take the stress of hearing their kids scream or cry, so I even draw a graph — it's gonna spike up right here. Knowing what to expect helps them stay with their superpower. Suddenly, if they hang in there, the child takes a breath and calms down. The behaviors may subside for a bit or even spike again, but like a brush fire, they eventually burn out. You're not providing the fuel of attention.

Cool it down – The goal is to avoid escalation. My mom would explain, "This will be good for you, and you'll be making new friends." She would divert me into the positive parts of the experience, but she wouldn't give it much attention. So I wouldn't be in the escalated state. She would always wait until my outburst subsided, and from that place, I could hear what she had to say.

> *When the parent stops feeding tantrums and behaviors, they expect magic. But, the initial patience power produces an even bigger flare-up.*

That's what got me through the transition. It was like battery polarity: Her polarity would be calm when I was charged. My charge would come at her calm state, then subside, and we could have a conversation that would help me accept the uncertainties. I took in the fact that it would be good for me little by little.

Extinction – The professional term for waiting for the

fire to burn out is extinction. Extinction is when you no longer reinforce previously reinforced behaviors by giving your child what they want, such as through attention (examples: peer attention, parent attention, trying to get out of a task, reinforcing by giving them what they want). You will see a spike in behavior once you implement extinction. Fire alarms and sirens don't put out a fire. It is the cool water of calm that extinguishes the blaze.

What does this look like in real life?

Neutral face – When working with families, we use our resting neutral face to apply the cool water of calm. If we show alarm, we are fanning the flames. If you were a superhero, your superpower would be your resting neutral face. I practice it so much that my coworkers created a coffee mug glazed with a resting neutral face. You can practice it in front of a mirror or when you're highly annoyed talking to some bureaucrat on the phone.

You might argue, "Isn't practicing a neutral face just another kind of attention?" Absolutely, yes. It takes work to maintain a neutral face. You're still attending to the situation with your full Spidey-Sense. The neutral face represents the lack of fuel you are giving to the amped-up person opposite you.

People express concern that *Patience Power*, and neutral face seem heartless. "This feels robotic," they'll say. I answer that you're not being heartless or robotic, and you're not in reaction or manipulating. If anything, the patient place creates space for genuine compassion — for your child and yourself. It takes you to the no-fault zone where you can witness your children's behaviors as completely innocent. They're only navigating the experience of their social world. They are exploring their environment based on what they have and what they've been given.

When I see a child having a tantrum, I feel that compassion. I feel that this is innocent and normal, and it's okay.

The patient place – It's impossible to keep the ship on an even keel because, like wind and waves, life is full of uncertainties. We can't anticipate the distractions in a store, the crazy energy at a party, or even the heightened emotions during the holidays. But we work to keep our environments balanced, structured, and even-keeled by staying in the patient place.

I'm not some super ninja with *Patience Power*; sometimes, my inner child still rebels. For example, my husband has picked up my neutral-ninja strategies, and uses them to good effect. He likes to practice a slow, contemplative ritual in the morning — brew coffee, check the financial markets, maybe read a chapter in a book. When I get up, it's go-go-go. I try to get his attention: "Honey, I've got a meeting in 15 minutes. Blah-blah-blah, you've gotta hear this now!"

He's not ready for intense conversations about kids, schooling, and the tutor. What does he do? He practices a neutral face.

Like any child, I experience my spike because my husband is no longer giving me attention when I want. I settle down because I know he's waiting for the storm to calm.

So, where's the payoff? Is *Patience Power* just a tool to manage family dynamics, or are you bestowing a lasting gift to your children?

Someday, the power might go out while you're cooking a turkey on Thanksgiving, and your kids will see how you pivot. "Let's go to the park for a while. And if we eat turkey at midnight, that will be fun, too." Instead of letting disappointment set in, I immediately rebalance the situation and redirect my kids to a new adventure.

You want your children to be able to weather the uncertainties in life. Children growing up during a pandemic are getting a master's class in resilience. If they have to move to a new home suddenly, get fired from a job, grieve the death of a loved one, or feel any sense of disappointment, they might need that resilience in the future.

By turning late-night turkey into a fun experience, they taste the moment of uplift waiting to be discovered in every bummer — even when mom and dad are acting like a rock.

Now, enough seriousness of the neutral face; let's move on to the *Fun Zone*!

Is patience power just a tool to manage family dynamics, or are you bestowing a lasting gift to your children?

You want your children to be able to weather the uncertainties in life.

The Fun Zone is a no-blame zone. If the Fun Zone had an entrance sign, it would read:

"All Ye Who Enter are Innocent."

Fun Zone

When I was a child, a 52-inch child to be exact, my father took me to ride Autopia at Disneyland. Autopia lets kids drive gas-powered mini cars around a scenic landscape of roadways, tunnels, and bridges. Pretty cool. My dad is a car nut, so he was extremely intent on me driving – like, "Maria, we're gonna make this happen."

There was only one problem. The minimum height to drive at Autopia is 54 inches. A normal parent would have said, "No problem; you can ride with me," or "Let's come back next year." But not my dad; we were partners in crime.

"Suck in your gut, shoulders back, stretch your spine. You got this!" And just like that, I was behind the wheel.

If you're wondering why a book on parenting would encourage lawless behavior, kids need to know that you're still a kid, too – that you know your way around the *Fun*

Zone.

My dad was so excited. After Autopia with its boring safety rails, I always wanted to drive a car. When I discovered one of our neighborhood friends had an old golf cart we could ride in at the park, I would drive that little cart on the park path for hours. By high school, I volunteered to drive the carpool in Los Angeles traffic to and from school every day, and I loved every minute I could get behind the wheel – all because of my dad.

Non-contingent reinforcement – I didn't know it at the time (and he certainly didn't know it), but he was practicing what we call in the world of behavioral health non-contingent reinforcement (I prefer non-contingent pairing)– but for this chapter, it's the *Fun Zone*. I didn't think of his antics as pairing – not non-contingent or the other kind; my dad was just fun to be around. He would drive us to school on his way to work, always eating an apple. The routine went: "Seat belts, check. Backpacks, check. Apple core, check!" And with that, he carefully deposited the apple core into the console. It seems silly, but we loved the theatricality he brought to mundane life.

When we got out of the car, he'd pull away with a

flourish, "Have a good day at school; I gotta go fight the dragons." As I headed to class, I imagined him fighting real dragons – that we were both going to fight the good fight – me versus math and he, as a developer, fighting lenders, insurers, and city planners.

The emotional barometer – My dad's upbeat nature served as a barometer, one that I watched closely – I wanted to see his cheery smile all the time.

I once asked my dad, "Dad, why aren't you smiling?"

He suddenly realized that my *"total recall"* was recording everything.

"Oh, I was fighting the dragons today, but you know, the sun will come out tomorrow."

Just like that, he would change gears and re-enter the *Fun Zone* with us kids.

Wanting non-stop smiles from my working parents with four kids was too much for me to expect. Today, when I play my mental memory tape from my childhood, I see how chaotic our home life was. Instead of silencing us to calm down, my dad might jump on the coffee table and shake his legs and knees in a funny dance.

"Hey everyone," he shouted, "let's all do the constipation!"

We bent over laughing, picked up the spirit, and danced the constipation. Even my no-nonsense mom joined in.

Looking back, dancing the constipation dance was my dad's superpower. He could turn on a dime and enter

the *Fun Zone*. He wasn't manipulative or in a place of denial. He kept that buoyancy in his heart. I would watch his face for emotional cues – he would always lift the mood when things got tense.

The *Fun Zone* is not about getting silly or pumping the energy. It's a heartfelt place where you feel happy to have a family and love your kids.

The no-blame zone – The *Fun Zone* is a no-blame zone. If the *Fun Zone* had an entrance sign, it would read, "All Ye Who Enter are Innocent." I'm not going to pretend – kids act out, or worse, they become teens with perennial chips on their shoulders. You sense their negative vibe, "Get away from me; I don't wanna talk to you." As a human being, your natural reaction is to withhold attention from a sullen kid.

Here comes the superpower: Just because your child said something that made you uncomfortable, you can't shut down for a day or a week. You have to find the reservoir of buoyancy in your heart. Maybe you can talk about something super positive or compliment your child at dinnertime.

Money in the bank – Spending time in the *Fun Zone* is like putting money in the bank. The day will come when you have to lay down the law. Then, it will be easier, like my mom and dad sending me to private high school, to speak firmly and seriously from a connected place.

I'm not sugar-coating the *Fun Zone*, as I've been on the receiving end from a hateful child. When I was teaching middle school, some kids hated my guts. They pretty much wanted me dead. They didn't actually know me; this was how they reacted in general. At the time, I was getting my degree, taking lots of notes, and absorbing data. I asked another more experienced teacher about working with a hateful child. She paused.

> *Spending time in the Fun Zone is like putting money in the bank. The day will come when you have to lay down the law.*

"You have to find a way to reinforce the child," she replied.

"Okay…" I replied unsurely, "but how, what?" Then I protested. "The kid is a monster."

"Reinforce them for sitting, breathing, for whatever," my teacher calmly answered. "You can always find something to praise."

Find something to praise – I was still young myself and not too happy with her answer. So, I took it as a challenge. How can I get on my students' wavelengths? I was on FM, and they were on AM – our receivers were not picking up each other's signals. I needed to shift. Instead of seeing their behaviors as transgressions, I needed to see them as innocent. They were in a *Fun Zone* of their own making.

Non-contingent pairing – When my college professors introduced the concept of non-contingent pairing, a little light went on. It's like Bluetooth pairing -- you have to establish a connection between two devices. And like Bluetooth, I wasn't "discoverable" by my students. The secret was for me to become curious about their world. Whether it was dirty lyrics, extreme hair colors, skateboard wheels, or obscure video games, a world lay hidden in front of my eyes, and I needed to pair with it.

I discovered how, with pairing, the parent or caregiver associates with items and activities the child prefers. It could be blowing giant soap bubbles, making popcorn, banging on drums, shooting squirt guns, creating TikToks, or driving go-karts. In clinician language, you're creating positive reinforcement through non-contingent pairing. Non-contingent means no threat, no deal, no quid pro quo – just freely-given enjoyment of another human being. For this chapter, non-contingent pairing means you're entering the *Fun Zone*.

A sack of good vibes – Success is impossible without pairing – especially for a parent hoping to teach a child, achieve compliance, or change behaviors. You want the child to associate you with happy situations and moments of joy – like the constipation dance. Instead playing the enforcer, you carry a Santa sack filled with good vibes, emotional warmth, and fun. You don't need to say ho-ho-

ho – your warmth and smile function as cues to listen up because mom and dad have something the child wants. Kids tune into your mood, just like me when I asked, "Dad, why aren't you smiling?"

But pairing is not bringing a Santa sack of baseballs if your child doesn't want to play catch. Pushing them on the swing might be a vestibular nightmare for some kids. Misguided pairing usually interrupts a child who's engrossed in natural play. It also misses cues of immediate needs or offers tasks that create discomfort. The child's unwillingness to pair can look like laziness or defiance. Raising your voice to interact only makes it worse. Even singing the alphabet in a sweet and playful voice, "A-B-C-D," while looking expectantly for the child to say "E," places a demand.

Success is impossible without pairing. Instead playing the enforcer, you carry a Santa sack filled with good vibes, emotional warmth and fun.

Pairing begins with your face – "Wanna make some popcorn?" Wait for the child to make eye contact, and then connect through a smile. You can pair with warmth, friendliness, excitement, or soothing in your voice. Be aware that treats like juice or a snack can be effective but can also fail as reinforcements if the child expects a sweet or it's used as a reward for behavior. To this day, the pairing tactics my parents used 40 years ago prove to be effective.

Pairing ideas with small children include:
- Give a thumbs-up or smile from across the room
- Snuggle next to them on the couch
- Pretend you are tigers on hands and knees
- Toss a Nerf ball while making eye contact
- Dance with your kids to a novelty song from your youth

The *Fun Zone* opens through non-contingent pairing – another word for unconditional love.

Pairing is free from demands – even subtle ones. If you're coloring together, "Color the water blue" is a demand. "Say mommy's name" is a demand. "How was school today?" is a demand. "Wanna go for a walk and get ice cream?" carries no demand.

What if the child is doing something unsafe or inappropriate? When you yell, "Johnny, get down from the ladder; it's not safe!" you associate your voice with bad, unsafe, and negative situations. If possible, move to the ladder and scoop Johnny down without making a fuss. The goal is to avoid becoming the Fount of Anger, but the truth is, we all get angry sometimes.

Here's a pairing story – My brilliant stepson was a master at stretching the truth – a trait I can't bear – even if it would make him a brilliant politician. Once, when we were traveling, I turned to him in the car, "You didn't put any deodorant on."

"How do you know if I did or didn't," he retorted.

"I taught middle school boys. I know."

The next morning, I reminded, "Make sure you put deodorant on today."

"I forgot my deodorant. It's at home."

Naturally, he was lying. I hated when middle-schoolers lied to me, so now I'm angry. I didn't want to blow up and spoil the road trip, so I cooled down and let it go. After ten minutes, I told my husband, "He lied to me, and I'm angry. We have to teach him."

Inside, I knew he didn't want to lie intentionally. He's just making an underarm detour of convenience, plus he knew I was on to him. So, I told him, "Dude, I'm teaching you to be honest. I did the same thing at your age. I threw parties when my parents were gone and told them I was out with friends."

"Really? You did that?"

Maybe I made a mistake giving him the idea that unauthorized parties in the house were cool, but we also established a pairing. Suddenly, we saw each other eye-to-eye with a level of trust. He saw that I knew the *Fun Zone*, too, and he wouldn't need to hide from me.

The moral here is that it's natural for kids to slip and slide around the full story and for parents to get angry and emotionally react. And when they do, they lose their neutral face. What's worse, all this negativity bleeds into the environment and extinguishes the *Fun Zone*. Because of *Total Recall*, you're modeling for your kids all the time. So if you can model positive, fun interactions more often than negative, you will be putting money into the *Fun Zone* bank.

Individual Time – My dad was super aware of the *Fun Zone* bank. Did he understand psychology, or was he just a fun-loving Irishman? Either way, he always accrued a positive cash flow. His secret was Individual Time with Dad.

We had individual days with our father – no small feat with four kids. Imagine a heaping dose of positive reinforcement that an Individual Day would give a child. My dad would take one of us to a *Fun Zone* park each weekend, making Individual Day highly coveted. We might drive go-karts, ride bikes to the pier, swim in the ocean, or get ice cream.

Once, during show-and-tell, I shared a story about my "dad-daughter date" with the class. The boys in the back of the class started snickering, like, "Eeeww, you went on a date with your dad." But I was proud of it and huffed, "Sorry you don't get to go on dates with your dad."

The "dates" became more elaborate as I got older – maybe to a nice dinner, a theater performance, or a car dealer to test drive cars. The activity didn't matter. If the coin of the realm is attention, I had my dad's total attention.

But now, I'm the adult, and it's my job to ignite my *Fun Zone* superpower with my stepson (thank goodness, I didn't lose my cool over the deodorant). Every summer, we swim out into the middle of a small volcanic lake near our home and sing songs – just he and I together. When it's not swimming weather, we feast on exotic sushi, go rock climbing, or even fight with Nerf swords.

Children want to please – Why is the *Fun Zone* so effective? In their hearts, children want to please. You become their source of positive reinforcement – the coin of the realm that your kid wants to work for. Who would prefer to live in a stress-filled Conflict Zone when it feels so good to live in the *Fun Zone*?

Years ago, I watched a police officer talk to a kid about following the law. "Son, you don't want to go to jail." Then he said something that, coming from a cop, blew my mind. He talked about feelings. The officer said, "You feel really good when you follow the rules." More than the threat of punishment, feeling good can motivate behavior.

Non-contingent reinforcement – Laughter, smiling, and dad time made us "feel really good." It's called non-contingent reinforcement – non-contingent because you don't have to earn it. It's freely there because you're two human beings who love and support each other. It's a parent superpower, but also a child superpower – one that ignites in the heart of the child for the parent.

The shift from the blame zone to the *Fun Zone* takes time. It might take a year for you to make that shift. But once it happens, you begin to see innocence where you used to see misbehavior. Situations become less about you and more about your child's natural development.

The sweetest form of sugar – Someday, you may become a grandparent. Grandparents give their grandkids sugar – ice cream, cookies, cake, and candy. It's not healthy, but I never had one negative interaction with my grandmother. She lived down the street from us, so we hung out a lot. She was a complete joy, and made the pairing process effortless with all that sugar. But we're parents, so we can't give kids sugar all the time – preferably, rarely.

What we can give is the sweetest sugar of all, and that is love.

The next step isn't to try out some *Fun Zone* activity with your child – it's to find the fun place in your heart. This shift might take a year, but hopefully, it will take less time than that.

Why? Because you're two human beings, who love each other.

The shift from the blame zone to the Fun Zone takes time. It might take a year for you to make that shift.

But once it happens, you begin to see innocence where you used to see misbehavior.

What we put into the chalice for our children are not teachings, precepts, or how-tos.

The chalice is filled with your being. It's the feeling you give your child that someone has their back no matter what.

People Presents

In the 1970s, passionate Grateful Dead fans began traveling to as many shows as their funds and fuel would allow. These "Deadheads" would sell tie-dye T-shirts, veggie burritos, and illicit substances from the hippie camps that popped up around the venues to support their concert lifestyle. A sprawling community developed, all determined to stay in the Grateful Dead vibe. Before long, another generation of loyal fans – Phish Heads – began to follow another band, Phish, in roughly the same manner.

What does this have to do with me? Rather than spending my youth following a counter-culture jam band, I traveled from concert to concert following a guy from Australia who played solo, fingerstyle acoustic guitar.

You should be asking, "Maria, there is no shortage of solo acoustic guitar players in the United States; why did you follow Tommy Emmanuel?"

Tommy is an extraordinary guitarist. Some critics say it would take three musicians, or more, to do what Tommy does solo. I could have followed Jeff Beck or Ry Cooder if I was seeking a superb guitarist, but Tommy's "People Presence" – or for this chapter, *People Presents* – created a solid fan-to-artist bond.

My Tommy journey began when I was learning to play guitar. My guitar teacher said, "Maria, Tommy Emmanuel's in town. You need to see him play!"

Having no idea exactly what I was in store for, I bought a ticket and then saw a "Meet-and-Greet" option, so I got that, too. It didn't cost extra – I guess Tommy liked to meet and greet.

After the show, I gathered with the other fans; I was just a nobody, but Tommy looked into my eyes with a depth of kindness that awakened a profound feeling of *People Presents*. I still carry this palpable sense to this day. Having enjoyed the experience, I went to the next day's show, and he remembered my name. I'm thinking, aren't you too famous for little people like me?

A three-day break followed, and I saw Tommy play again. At this point, he was just easy and comfortable to be around. It was a small venue, so we hung out and had a beer while he tuned his guitar.

I never missed one of Tommy's shows when he came to town until it was clear that my super fan era was drawing to a close; my career loomed. I approached Tommy fondly at my last concert, gave him my card, and said, "If you ever need anything, feel free to reach out."

A year later, an email appeared in my inbox – from Tommy! "Hey, Maria. I'm on tour in Germany, and I found your card in my luggage. I'm just reaching out to say hello." This may not mean much to you, but for me, it could have been from Eric Clapton or Paul McCartney.

It's been about ten years since that email. Last week Tommy was in town, and there was no way I would miss his show. I walked up to him after the show, and to my surprise, he gave me a big embrace. Connecting deeply, he asked, "Maria, are you still taking care of autism in the world?"

"Yes, Tommy. I haven't given up," I answered, feeling a little giddy. "Just like you are inspiring millions with your music."

Tommy smiled, maintaining eye contact the whole time, a signature trait of the charisma so many of his fans appreciate, "We're all connected," he said. "We're doing this together."

You may take this as Maria's gushy girl fandom, but Tommy is one of my teachers. When he talks to me, he makes me feel like I'm the only person in the room. I learned this superpower

> *Tommy smiled, maintaining eye contact the whole time, "We're all connected," he said. "We're doing this together."*

of *People Presents* from Tommy, and I use it in my dealings with others. Tommy may be a musician, but people come first in his life. And when you're with him, you feel that he is there to bestow a gift from his depth as a person – a *People Present*.

People Presents are invisible gifts that are transmitted from soul to soul. Having read the book, you know the *People Presents* I received from my parents. Here are a few:

- **Chapter One**: The rich *Structure Zone* that bonded our family at dinner

- **Chapter Two**: My *Delayed Gratification* from two hours of TV per week

- **Chapter Three**: Learning how to *Choose the Right Bait* through the power of attention

- **Chapter Four**: The *Total Recall* awakened by my mother's purposeful, non-reactive superpower

- **Chapter Five**: My success at an all-girls high school from my parents' *Patience Power*

- **Chapter Six**: My coveted *Fun Zone* day with my dad at Autopia

- **Chapter Seven**: And now, how I learned to give and receive *People Presents*

Presents from Mom and Dad – All seven chapters speak to the remarkable presents I received from my parents. I have absorbed these presents and leveraged them into my career and relationships. I would be painting an inaccurate picture to suggest that growing up in a large, noisy, Italian family gave me a leg up in the world. In a talkative family, we talk at each other without really listening. Very few *People Presents* are given or received without listening.

When I was a teenager, I joked, "When me and my friend are on the phone, it's like two people talking to each other, but no one is listening."

> *People Presents are the superpower of listening.*

People Presents are the superpower of listening.

I first learned the meaning of listening from the priest who celebrated the wedding ceremony of my husband and me. He shared, "This is how you receive what someone has to give." Then he placed one open hand into the other like he was forming a chalice. With that gesture, I could feel his presence. He taught me how to give to the other person by listening – to a client, a peer, or a family member. It's an expression of being invested in them. I don't know if people see my hands under the table, but I gesture that way in meetings.

I didn't always have this superpower. I could barely wait my turn to talk about my day at the dinner table. And remember my little brother Mikey? He had to stand on his chair to get attention. As a teenager, I couldn't stop talking – that's what teens do. When I attended Columbia University, my professor picked up on my know-it-all, talkative nature. "Maria, I need you to pretend you never went to Gonzaga University and didn't get that master's degree – just throw it out."

I was thinking, what the heck! I just graduated with my master's degree, now I'm working on a credential and continuing my graduate studies, and you're telling me to forget everything! But I remembered the priest and the attitude of opening my hands into a chalice. One of the more important things I learned in graduate school was approaching each situation with a clean slate.

Opening your hands is like pairing – You can see challenging behavior as innocent and an expression of real needs by listening.

When the pandemic disrupted every sort of relationship, it also created an opportunity to experience real needs and appreciate people as gifts. Suddenly, our therapy practice was forced to switch completely to telehealth. It takes a lot of attention to stay connected during a Zoom meeting, and attention is in short supply with kids.

Contrary to what we expected, we had tremendous success with teenagers on telehealth. Why is that? We expected them to be distracted by the myriad things in the room. Unlike a group on Zoom, our telehealth sessions offered a one-on-one relationship. Like all people, these kids wanted to connect with another human being – and there we were, eye to eye, screen to screen.

Before each new client, we would get a written assessment of the problematic behaviors that brought them to our program. We did not see these behaviors during the session, which freed us to focus on the interaction and interpersonal skills and build from that. It became clear how telehealth forced us to talk with the person and become more present with each other.

The kids had an agenda, and like everyone, they needed someone to confide in who was on their wavelength. They came through our digital front door starved for that connection – for a *People Present*.

> *Opening your hands is like pairing. You can see challenging behavior as innocent and an expression of real needs by listening.*

Suddenly, we were pairing with them through telehealth, and wow, this feels good. The reported behaviors were not evident, suggesting that the child was using behaviors to get what he wanted. And what he wanted was attention.

Implementing telehealth to meet clients during a pandemic allowed us to reach out in a new and powerful way.

A co-regulated nervous system – Our children open their hearts and minds, trusting that what they receive from their family and the world will meet their needs. When that open-hearted purity is not met in love, they register alarm. They tighten, react, and exhibit behaviors that are not misdeeds. Instead of being met, their alarms go off. They seek safety and a calm, co-regulated nervous system.

My dog, Emma, is also an obedient and loving co-regulator. Scientists understand how having a companion like Emma, who receives you with total acceptance, can keep your heart rate at a calm level. That's why service

animals not only support the blind but also help people with autism. They may reduce anxiety or agitation with a calming action. The dog might lean against the child or gently lay across their lap.

Our pets have a lot to teach us. Emma draws from her chalice of total acceptance to help me open my heart and settle my nervous system. She wags, frolics, snuggles, and follows my lead in play. If I want to play ball, she pairs perfectly by playing my silly game until I want to move on to tug. Best of all, Emma provides non-contingent reinforcement throughout the day – often in the form of a lick.

Emma can't help with my homework or explain why I won't be attending public high school, but she draws from her instinct to serve. As a parent, you have more tricks up your sleeve than Emma and, importantly, more lived experience (but unfortunately, more responsibility, stress, worry, and uncertainty). Like my mom, who threatened to leave Olive Garden on the strength of her conviction, you also have many gifts – *People Presents* – to give to your children.

Maybe you served in the military, excelled in sports, or won the science fair. These successes form the fabric of who you are. Conversely, you may have faced major hardships, had parents who divorced, or suffered a childhood disease. These also helped form your true strength.

The greatest gift of all – What we put into the chalice for our children are not teachings, precepts, or how-tos. The chalice is filled with your being. It's the feeling you give your child that someone has their back no matter what. When the child knows that he is not alone and that his parents and caregivers are looking out for his best interest, this is the greatest of all superpowers – your *People Presents*.

As a parent, you are on a sacred mission – With two hands open, you transmit your presence and listen to your child's needs. You may feel life shoved you into a parenting role without the skills or fortitude required – especially if your kids behave in ways you never expected. I work with many families whose kids are newly diagnosed. These parents don't realize that they have

a wellspring of untapped superpowers that will be a godsend in the journey ahead.

We all have these powers, and, like Superman, you only discover how to melt steel or stop bullets in a critical moment. You discover your neutral face or how to see children in an innocent light when all hell is breaking loose.

What's difficult today will become easier tomorrow. One thing is certain – that your relationship with your children is sacred. Even when you are 70 and they are 40, the chalice your children bring to you will still be held open, waiting to receive your *People Presents*.

What's difficult today will become easier tomorrow.

One thing is certain — that your relationship with your children is sacred.

Acknowledgments

To my husband: Dan, you are my number one man. I remember when we first locked eyes when I was 15 years old. Thank you for making me happier than I ever dreamed I could be. You are still the one.

My parents: You have and always will be my most influential teachers. I cherish every lesson you've taught me. Thank you for your unconditional love throughout my life and for raising me using positive parenting practices.

My siblings, Karen, Brian, and Michael:

The greatest gift our parents gave us was each other.

My older sister Karen: Thank you for putting up with me copying everything you did as a kid and for your continued love and support through our adult years.

My older brother Brian: I am grateful for you being a constant rock for me. I also greatly appreciate the work you did on editing this book.

My younger brother Michael: My other pea in the pod – you bring out the joy in my life! I cherish our soul sibling friendship every single day.

Uncle Don: You are a true godfather – naturally versed with parental superpowers. All of your godchildren aspire to embody your people presence.

Uncle Val and Aunt Adrienne: For your unconditonal love and support, and for modeling what a selfless, caring, and loving marriage looks like.

Bruce Miller: Your contributions to the creation of this book brought me into a whole new world of opportunity to teach others. Thank you for your dedication.

Gene Baz: Your artistic talent behind the playful and engaging illustrations bring the pages to life.

Dr. Bryan Davey: I'm so grateful to have you as my mentor and that I still get to work with you and learn from your extraordinary leadership.

Paul Boynton: Your insights have guided my journey. I appreciate you and your *Begin with Yes* community of positive, creative, and loving people.

Kelly Stafford: One of the world's best BCBAs and my trusted editor. Thank you for your insightful feedback and support of this journey.

My parents-in-law, Maggi and Larry, my brothers-in-law, Sergio and Tim, and my sisters-in-law, Lindy and Kristina: Thank you for hanging with me in all the zones, structured and otherwise.

My brilliant team at Wynne Solutions: Thank you for putting all of these ideas into action.

To my kids, relatives, friends, and everyone whose story appears in these pages: You have been my village and one I would choose over and over again.

Author Bio

Dr. Maria Gilmour has worked professionally with families for the past 20 years as a parent educator and a board-certified behavior analyst.

Dr. Gilmour works with parents and families, teachers, educational leaders, and school administrators in both public and non-public programs for children with special needs. She is well known for her creative approach to cross-disciplinary collaboration.

She feels that a child is best served when parents and family members, educators, and therapists work together to support the specific needs of a child. Dr. Gilmour has worked as a consultant for families and educational programs all over the world through telehealth solutions.

In addition to her current role as Chief Executive Officer of Wynne Solutions, Dr. Gilmour also works as Chief Clinical Officer of Gemiini Systems, a discrete video modeling program for individuals building language and social skills.

SEVEN SUPERPOWERS

1. Structure Zone – Provide as much predictability, consistency, and follow through as possible.

2. Delayed Gratification – Create comfort with uncertainty by modeling patience.

3. Choosing the Right Bait – Watch your child for shifting interests and follow their lead.

4. Total Recall – Remember that your child is recording your actions and reactions at all times.

5. Patience Power – Cool it down and model resilience with your neutral face.

6. Fun Zone – Enter the no-blame zone where "All who enter are innocent!"

7. People Presents – Let your child know and feel that you have their back no matter what.

Made in the USA
Coppell, TX
19 May 2023

17013972R10066